Busy People

By Babs Bell Hajdusiewicz

Illustrated by Laura Cornell

ScottForesman

A Division of HarperCollinsPublishers

Busy people change the tire.

Busy people fight the fire.

Busy people stop the cars.

Busy people play guitars.

Busy people sweep the street.

Busy people cook and eat.

Busy people with work to do.
Busy people just like you.